Applying the Standards:
Evidence-Based Reading
Grade 1

Credits
Content Editor: Jeanette M. Ritch, MS. Ed.
Copy Editor: Elise Craver

Visit *carsondellosa.com* for correlations to Common Core, state, national, and Canadian provincial standards.

Carson Dellosa Education
PO Box 35665
Greensboro, NC 27425 USA
carsondellosa.com

ISBN 978-1-4838-1459-9
03-042191151

Table of Contents

Introduction

The purpose of this book is to engage students in close reading while applying the standards. The Common Core reading and language strands are reflected in the interactive questions that follow each passage.

The lessons are intended to help students not only comprehend what they read superficially, but also to help them read complex texts closely and analytically. Students need to get involved deeply with what they are reading and use higher-order thinking skills to reflect on what they have read.

On the following activity pages, students will read a variety of literature and informational passages. These are brief but lend themselves to more complex thinking. Given the opportunity to study shorter texts, students can better practice the higher-level skills they need to closely read more demanding texts.

Each selection is followed by text-dependent questions. Students are prompted to pay attention to how a text is organized, to solve the question of why the author chose specific words, to look for deeper meaning, and to determine what the author is trying to say.

Use the included rubric to guide assessment of student responses and further plan any necessary remediation. The art of close reading is an invaluable skill that will help students succeed in their school years and beyond.

Common Core Alignment Chart

Use this chart to plan your instruction, practice, or remediation of a specific standard. To do this, first choose your targeted standard; then, find the pages listed on the chart that correlate to the standard.

Common Core State Standards*		Practice Pages
Reading Standards for Literature		
Key Ideas and Details	1.RL.1–1.RL.3	5–26
Craft and Structure	1.RL.4–1.RL.6	5–8, 10–19, 21, 24–26
Integration of Knowledge and Ideas	1.RL.7, 1.RL.9	7–9, 11, 19, 22, 23, 26
Range of Reading and Level of Text Complexity	1.RL.10	Each reading passage can be adapted to exercise this standard.
Reading Standards for Informational Text		
Key Ideas and Details	1.RI.1–1.RI.3	27–62
Craft and Structure	1.RI.4– 1.RI.6	27–30, 32–38, 40–43, 47, 48, 52, 53, 56, 57, 59, 61, 62
Integration of Knowledge and Ideas	1.RI.7– 1.RI.9	33, 35, 39–43, 46, 49, 50, 53, 57, 59, 62
Range of Reading and Level of Text Complexity	1.RI.10	Each reading passage can be adapted to exercise this standard.
Reading Standards: Foundational Skills		
Fluency	1.RF.4	Each reading passage can be adapted to exercise this standard.
Language Standards		
Vocabulary Acquisition and Use	1.L.4–1.L.6	6–8, 10–13, 16–19, 21, 24–27, 30, 32–38, 40–42, 47, 48, 52, 57, 59, 61

Reading Comprehension Rubric

Use this rubric as a guide to assess students' written work. It can also be offered to students to help them check their work or as a tool to show your scoring.

4	_____ Offers insightful reasoning and strong evidence of critical thinking _____ Makes valid, nontrivial inferences based on evidence in the text _____ Skillfully supports answers with relevant details from the text _____ Gives answers that indicate a complete understanding of the text _____ Gives answers that are easy to understand, clear, and concise _____ Uses conventions, spelling, and grammar correctly
3	_____ Offers sufficient reasoning and evidence of critical thinking _____ Makes inferences based on evidence in the text _____ Supports answers with details from the text _____ Gives answers that indicate a good understanding of the text _____ Gives answers that are easy to understand _____ Uses conventions, spelling, and grammar correctly most of the time
2	_____ Demonstrates some evidence of critical thinking _____ Makes incorrect inferences or does not base inferences on evidence in the text _____ Attempts to support answers with information from the text _____ Gives answers that indicate an incomplete understanding of the text _____ Gives answers that are understandable but lack focus _____ Gives answers containing several errors in conventions, spelling, and grammar
1	_____ Demonstrates limited or no evidence of critical thinking _____ Makes no inferences _____ Does not support answers with details from the text _____ Gives answers that indicate little to no understanding of the text _____ Gives answers that are difficult to understand _____ Gives answers with many errors in conventions, spelling, and grammar

Name _____

Read. Then, answer the questions.

Sarah's Camping Trip

Sarah went on a camping trip. She went with her family. They put their supplies into the car. They took a tent, three sleeping bags, three backpacks, and a cooler.

Sarah and her mother bought food at the grocery store. They put the food in the cooler. Her father put ice on top of the food to keep it cold.

Her father put up the tent. Sarah helped him. Her mother made dinner. Sarah helped her too.

They sang songs around the campfire. Her mother told stories. Then, they made graham cracker with marshmallow sandwiches.

Sarah liked sleeping in a tent. She had a great time on her camping trip.

1. What did Sarah's family bring on the trip?

_____

2. How did they keep the food cold?

_____

3. Where did they sleep?

_____

☀ Reflect

Will Sarah take another camping trip soon? Why do you think so?

_____

_____

_____

_____

_____

Name _____

Read. Then, answer the questions.

Birthday Candles

Birthday candles are on the cake.
How many candles does it take?

One for baby sister Jane.
Three for little brother Cain.

Five for my funny cousin, Lee.
Almost seven just for me.

Nine for my sister. Her name is Gail.
Ten for my oldest brother, Dale.

We saved a **bunch** for Mom and Dad.
Grandma needed all we had.

Birthday candles are on the cake.
How many candles does it take?

1. What is a *bunch*?

_____

2. Describe Lee.

_____

3. Why are so many candles on the cake?

_____

_____

☀ Reflect

How is this birthday cake different from most?

_____

_____

_____

_____

_____

Name _____

Read. Then, answer the questions.

Grayson and the Dragon

Once upon a time, Grayson wanted to play with a dragon. So, he went to find one.

Soon, he came to an old, gray palace. Grayson shouted, "Is there a dragon home?"

"Yes," answered the dragon. The dragon began to huff and puff. He blew until all of his fire was gone.

The dragon began to cry. "What good is a dragon with no fire? Besides, I am not a mean dragon. I am a playful dragon. I just want to have fun."

"Me too!" said Grayson. "Why don't you come home with me? We will play together." So, Grayson became **special**. He was the only kid with his own dragon.

1. Who is telling the story?

_____

2. What does *special* mean?

_____

3. What does the dragon look like?

_____

☀ Reflect

How does the dragon feel about being different? How do you know?

_____

_____

_____

Name _____

Read. Then, answer the questions.

Playing Dress-Up

Ana likes to play dress-up. She likes to dress as a bride. Ana puts on a long, white dress and **drapes** a pretty shawl on her head. She even has some roses. Sometimes, she puts on her big sister's dance outfit. Then, she does a dance. Ana also thinks it is fun to be a clown. She puts on her dad's big shoes and colors her nose red.

Ana likes playing Mom best. She dresses in her mom's clothes. She takes her basket and shops for food in the kitchen pantry. Her doll is always her baby. She feeds her baby. Then, she sings her baby to sleep.

Playing dress up is a lot of fun.

1. What does *drapes* mean?

_____

2. How does Ana dress like a clown?

_____

3. How does Ana feel about playing Mom?

_____

 **Reflect**

Why do you think Ana likes playing Mom best?

_____

_____

Name _____

Read. Then, answer the questions.

A Hot Summer Day

It was a hot summer day. "This is a good day to be lazy. I will lie in the shade of the apple tree," said Bill.

Soon, Katie came skipping by. "What are you doing?" she asked.

"Oh, nothing," replied Bill.

"I think I will do nothing too," said Katie. She sat down next to Bill.

They saw an ant pulling a big leaf. A ladybug flew onto Katie's hand. A grasshopper hopped by. A bee landed on a flower. "It is fun doing nothing," said Bill and Katie.

1. What does Bill do?

_____

_____

2. Where did Katie sit?

_____

3. What did Bill and Katie see?

_____

_____

Reflect

Why do Bill and Katie say, "It is fun doing nothing"?

_____

_____

_____

Name _____

Read. Then, answer the questions.

It Is Time

It is time for what?
It is time for time!
Whatever is time for?

It is time to go to bed.
It is time to wake up.
It is time to eat.

It is time to be good.
It is time to do your best.
It is time to learn.

It is time to go out.
It is time to come in.
It is time to be there.

It is time to grow up.
It is time to stay young.
Whatever your age, it is time.

It is your time to be.
It is my time for me.
Let's be friends—it is time.

1. In the poem, what does it mean to do your best?

_____

2. When is it time to learn?

_____

3. Why is it time to be friends?

_____

Reflect

What times are mentioned in the poem? Why?

_____

_____

_____

Name _____

Read. Then, answer the questions.

Denise and Her Kite

Denise got a new kite. It was blue and red with white spots.

Denise wanted to fly her kite. She went outside. The wind was blowing. She went up a hill. She ran fast down the hill. Her kite went up and up, high in the sky. Denise had fun flying her new kite.

1. Describe Denise's kite.

_____

2. What was it like outside?

_____

3. Where did her kite go?

_____

 **Reflect**

Why did Denise have fun?

_____

_____

Read. Then, answer the questions.

Toad Floats On a Boat

Cody loves to make things. Today, he made a boat from a bar of soap. He used a stick, rope, and some paper for the sail. Then, Cody took the boat to the pond. He wanted to see if it would float. He put the boat into the water. It floated! Cody was **proud**. Suddenly, a little toad jumped from the shore onto the boat. The toad sat happily on the boat.

1. What did Cody make?

_____

2. What does *proud* mean?

_____

3. Why was the toad happy?

_____

Reflect

Is this a story or fact? How do you know?

_____

_____

Name _____

Read. Then, answer the questions.

Uncle Rich

Uncle Rich always says,
"Children, choose one thing.
Anything you ask for,
That's the thing I'll bring."

Chad chose a choo-choo train.
Chase chose a chair.
Chang chose a chopper toy
That flies in the air.

Chelsea chose some chocolate.
Chuck chose a chestnut.
Chester chose checkers,
His favorite game.

Uncle Rich brought each child
That one favorite thing.
But, more than things,
It's **joy** that their favorite uncle brings.

1. What did Chang choose?

_____

2. Whose favorite game is checkers?

_____

3. What does *joy* mean?

_____

☀ Reflect

How does Uncle Rich bring more than things?

_____

_____

_____

Name _____

Read. Then, answer the questions.

Bob the Crossing Guard

Bob the crossing guard does his job. He helps us cross the street. Cars, buses, and trucks go by.

Bob the crossing guard holds up his hand and says, "Stop!" We cross the street. Thank you Bob, the crossing guard, for doing your job.

1. What is Bob's job?

_____

2. What kind of vehicles go by?

_____

3. Is this a story or fact? How do you know?

_____

✵ Reflect

Why is Bob's job important?

_____

_____

Name _____

Read. Then, answer the questions.

Megan the Vet

Megan is a vet. Vets help sick pets. Vets help pets get well. Some vets help big pets. Some vets help little pets.

A vet can wrap a dog's leg. A vet can mend a horse with a cut. A vet can fix a cat with no pep. A vet can help your pet too. Megan likes being a vet.

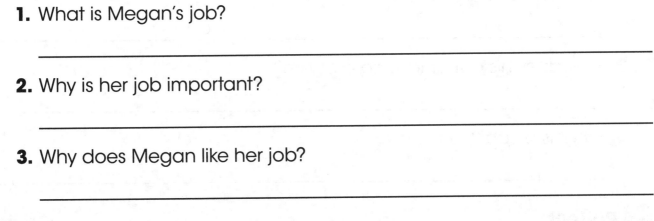

1. What is Megan's job?

_____

2. Why is her job important?

_____

3. Why does Megan like her job?

_____

 **Reflect**

How are vets the same as doctors?

_____

_____

Name _____

Read. Then, answer the questions.

Sparky

Sparky is the name of my new dog. Dad gave him to me as a gift. He is white with a black **spot** around one eye. I take care of him. I give him food and water. I made a warm place for him to sleep.

Sparky and I have fun. We play ball. I toss the ball. He brings it back. I hide from him. He finds me. We like to race. When I come home from school, he is there to meet me. It is fun having my own dog.

1. What does Sparky look like?

_____

2. How does his owner take care of him?

_____

3. What is a *spot*?

_____

 **Reflect**

How does the author feel about having a dog? How do you know?

_____

_____

Name _____

Read. Then, answer the questions.

Wave Rider

Nathan has a sailboat named *Wave Rider*. James is Nathan's **shipmate**. Nathan sails the boat. James keeps the boat clean and neat.

Nathan and James like to sail whenever they can. Today, they catch a big wave out to sea. Nathan brags about the perfect day. Suddenly, it starts to rain.

The sea is no longer safe. The wind seems to **scream**, "Race to shore!" Nathan and James sail the boat back to shore. They will wait to sail another day.

1. What is a *shipmate*?

_____

2. How does the wind *scream* at Nathan and James?

_____

3. Why do Nathan and James sail back to shore?

_____

☀ Reflect

How do Nathan and James work together?

_____

_____

Name _____

Read. Then, answer the questions.

The Hen and the Pig

Tad has a hen. The hen has 10 chicks. The hen and her chicks were in the pen. Tad fed the hen and her chicks.

Oh, no!

Tad's pig ran into the hen's pen. The hen and the chicks ran out. The pig ran fast after the hen. Tad ran fast after the pig.

What now?

Dad ran after the pig. Dad grabbed the pig. Dad put the pig in the pigpen. Tad fed the pig some **slop**.

Then, Tad ran after the hen and her chicks. Tad grabbed the hen. Tad put the hen in her pen. The chicks went too.

The pig is happy. The hen and her chicks are happy. Tim and his dad are happy.

1. What did Tad's pig do?

_____

2. What did Dad have to do to get the pig into the pigpen?

_____

3. What is *slop*?

_____

☀ Reflect

How does everyone feel by the end of the story? Why?

_____

_____

Name _____

Read. Then, answer the questions.

Pups and Cubs

Pups and cubs are little and cute. In fact, pups and cubs are **adorable**. Pups make good pets, but cubs do not.

Pups are baby dogs. They like to run. Cubs are baby bears. They like to run too. You can run with pups but not with cubs. A pup's mother would be glad if you ran with her pup. But, a cub's mother would be mad if you ran with her cub.

Pups and cubs like to tug. Pups are fun to play tug with, but a cub's tug can be too much! So, chose a pup for a pet, not a cub.

1. What does *adorable* mean?

_____

2. How would a pup's mother feel if you run with her pup?

_____

3. How would a cub's mother feel if you run with her cub?

_____

⁂ Reflect

Which animal makes a better pet, a pup or a cub? Why?

_____

_____

Name _____

Read. Then, answer the questions.

The Pot of Gold

One day, Josh went outside to play. He saw a big pot. "Where is the gold?" Josh asked. "Pots always have gold."

Josh looked for the gold. He stomped his foot. "Who has my gold?" he asked.

Suddenly, a little man appeared.

"You took my gold!" said Josh.

"No," said the little man. "You took my pot."

"This is your pot?" asked Josh.

"Yes," said the little man.

"I'm sorry. Here you go." Josh gave the little man his pot. The little man gave Josh some gold.

1. What did Josh see?

_____

2. Where was the gold?

_____

3. Compare Josh's feelings to the little man's feelings.

_____

_____

☀ Reflect

Did Josh's attitude change in the story? How?

_____

_____

_____

Name _____

Read. Then, answer the questions.

Dawn the Zookeeper

   Dawn is a zookeeper. Her job is to keep the animals in the zoo safe and happy. She cleans the cages and gives the animals clean straw. Last week, a hawk began to squawk. Dawn saw that it had a sore claw. She called a vet to fix the hawk's claw. Another time, two of the big cats had a **brawl** over food. One cat got a hurt paw. The other cat got a sore jaw. Dawn took care of the big cats. Dawn loves animals. Dawn loves her job.

1. What is Dawn's job?

_____

2. What does *brawl* mean?

_____

3. What happened to the two cats who had a brawl?

_____

✺ Reflect

Is this a story or fact? How do you know?

_____

_____

Name _____

Read. Then, answer the questions.

The Show

   Ruby and her friends had a music show. The show was in July. Judy played a tune on her flute. Hugo played the bugle. Luke marched in his new uniform. Susan danced in her cute tutu. Jan and Ruby played a duet on their lutes. Drew played his huge tuba to end the show. Ruby said that all of her friends were super!

1. When was the show?

_____

2. What did Judy play?

_____

3. What did Susan do?

_____

 **Reflect**

What did Ruby think of the show? How do you know?

_____

_____

Name _____

Read. Then, answer the questions.

Maria's Surprise

Maria woke up early. Mom and Dad were asleep. She wanted to surprise them. Maria dressed herself. She combed her hair and went downstairs.

Maria put cereal in two bowls. She added some milk. She made toast with jam. Maria put the food on a tray. She took it upstairs to Mom and Dad. They were surprised to have breakfast in bed.

1. Why did Maria wake up early?

_____

2. What kind of food did she make?

_____

3. Whom did she bring the tray to?

_____

☀ Reflect

How does the title fit the story?

_____

_____

Name _____

Read. Then, answer the questions.

Hide-and-Seek

"Will you play hide-and-seek?" Jose asked his mother.

"I do not have time. I have to find some tape," said Jose's mother.

"I will help," said Jose. He looked everywhere. He found his mother's tape in a pile on her desk.

"Will you play hide-and-seek?" Jose asked his brother.

"I do not have time. I have to find my kite," his brother said.

"I will help," Jose said. He looked everywhere. He found his brother's kite by the gate.

"Will you play hide-and-seek?" Jose asked his father.

"I do not have time. I have to find my rope," his father said.

"I will help," Jose said. He looked everywhere. He found his father's rope by the rake.

"Will you play hide-and-seek?" Jose asked his sister.

"I do not have time. I have to find my dime," his sister said.

"I will help," Jose said. He looked everywhere. He found his sister's dime behind the drapes.

"It is too bad no one has time to play hide-and-seek," laughed Jose.

1. What did Jose's mom need to find?

_____

2. What did Jose's brother need to find?

_____

3. What things did Jose find?

_____

Reflect

Did Jose get to play hide-and-seek? Why or why not?

_____

Name _____

Read. Then, answer the questions.

The Race

Sammy Snail was sad. He wanted to be in the big race, but he was too slow. Robbie Rabbit hopped over to Sammy Snail. "Why are you so sad?" he asked.

"I want to be in the big race!" cried Sammy Snail.

"Sammy Snail, you are too slow!" laughed Robbie Rabbit as he hopped down the road.

Kami Kangaroo saw Sammy Snail on her way to the race. "Why are you crying?" she asked.

"I am too slow to be in the big race!" sobbed Sammy Snail.

"Do not cry. I will help you," said Kami Kangaroo. She picked up Sammy Snail. She dropped him in her kangaroo pouch.

Soon, it was time for the big race. Robbie Rabbit and Kami Kangaroo raced together. As they hopped to the finish line, Kami Kangaroo took Sammy Snail out of her **pouch**. She set him across the finish line. Sammy Snail won the big race!

1. Why was Sammy Snail sad?

_____

2. What is a *pouch*?

_____

3. Who won the big race?

_____

☀ Reflect

Underline what Robbie Rabbit said to Sammy Snail. How did it make him feel?

_____

_____

Name _____

Read. Then, answer the questions.

My Dream

Last night, I had a dream about being an astronaut. As I fell asleep, I found myself counting, "Three, two, one, blast off!" I dreamed that I flew into space.

I landed on Mars first. I raced in the red **soil**, making dust clouds behind me. Next, I played leapfrog on the moons of Jupiter. Then, I flew around the rings of Saturn. Suddenly, I began spinning out of control. The next thing I knew, I was on my bedroom floor.

I hope my dream comes true someday.

1. What is *soil*?

_____

2. Where is the setting of this dream?

_____

3. What game did the dreamer play?

_____

 **Reflect**

Where did the dreamer land at the end of the dream? Why?

_____

_____

Name _____

Read. Then, answer the questions.

Gentle Giants

What would you do if your neck were 6 feet (1.83 m) long? What would you do if your legs were 6 feet long? What would you do if your neck and your legs were both 6 feet long? Then, you would be the tallest animal on Earth. You would be a giraffe.

Why is a giraffe so tall? Its height helps it reach the tops of trees. It eats the leaves at the tops of trees. The giraffe has a long black tongue. Its tongue is 18 inches (45.72 cm) long. The tongue helps it pull leaves off of the trees. A giraffe spends half of each day eating. A giraffe can eat just a few leaves at a time. Because it is so big, it eats about 75 pounds (34.02 kg) of food a day. It chews for a long time!

Adult giraffes are big. Other animals do not bother them. But, baby giraffes are small. Animals such as lions may try to hunt them. Mother giraffes have a way to **guard** their babies. One adult tends a group of babies. The other mothers go off to eat. If a lion comes close, the adult giraffe kicks it away.

1. How long is a giraffe's neck?

_____

2. What does a giraffe's tongue do?

_____

3. What does *guard* mean?

_____

 **Reflect**

Why are giraffes so tall?

_____

_____

Name _____

Read. Then, answer the questions.

What Is in a Cake?

Mom's Best White Cake

- 1 cup flour
- 1 cup sugar
- 1 teaspoon baking powder
- 1 teaspoon salt

- 1/2 cup butter
- 1 teaspoon vanilla
- 2 eggs

1. Preheat oven to 350°F.

2. Mix flour, sugar, baking powder, and salt.

3. In a separate bowl, cream together butter, vanilla, and eggs.

4. Add the flour mixture to the egg mixture and stir.

5. Pour batter into a greased cake pan. Bake for 30 minutes.

1. What is the name of the recipe?

_____

2. How much butter is needed?

_____

3. What temperature should the oven be?

_____

Reflect

Cake has a lot of ingredients. What ingredient is missing that people usually put on top of cakes?

_____

_____

Name _____

Read. Then, answer the questions.

Fire Safety Rules

1. Do not play with matches.

2. If you see a fire:
   Tell an adult. Call 9-1-1.

3. If you are in a burning house:
   Do not hide. Keep low.
   Break a window if you have to. Do not open a hot door.

4. If your clothes are on fire, stop, drop, and roll:
   Stop what you are doing.
   Drop to the floor or ground.
   Roll around until the fire is out.

5. Talk with your family about a fire escape plan.

1. What number do you call if you see a fire?

_____

2. What do you do if your clothes are on fire?

_____

3. Who makes a fire escape plan?

_____

Reflect

Why are the rules numbered?

_____

_____

_____

Name _____

Read. Then, answer the questions.

It Is Raining Cats and Frogs?

There was some **strange** weather on September 7, 1953. It happened in Leicester, Massachusetts. It rained frogs and toads! Kids could fill their pails with them! Some thought that the frogs and toads hopped out of a pond. They said the water was too high. But, others said they saw the frogs and toads fall from the sky. They found them on their roofs!

It is easy to see how a rain of animals from the sea or a lake could happen during a big storm. Sometimes, water from a pond is sucked up by huge wind. Then, it rains down somewhere else. Maybe that is what happened in Tiller's Ferry, South Carolina. It rained fish there in 1901. It rained trout and catfish. Fish were found in puddles in the fields.

Other places have had strange rain too. Rocks, golf balls, ducks, and candy have dropped from the sky! Keep your eyes open for the next interesting storm. It might be in your town!

1. What does *strange* mean?

_____

2. What happened in 1953?

_____

3. Which kinds of fish fell from the sky in 1901?

_____

 **Reflect**

Why does the title end with a question mark?

_____

_____

Name _____

Read. Then, answer the questions.

Frozen Delight

One night in 1905, an 11-year-old boy was mixing fruit drinks. His name was Frank Epperson. Frank added soda powder to the drinks. Frank lived in California. The weather report said that it would be cold that night. He wondered how his drink would taste if it was frozen. He put the glass outside. He left his wooden stirring stick in the glass.

In the morning, Frank looked at the glass. The drink was frozen solid! In the center was his wooden stick. Frank slid the treat out of the glass and held it by the stick. It was good!

Later, Frank made a machine that molded his snacks. He also made a machine to stamp his name on the sticks. Frank's son, George, thought of a name. He called Frank "Pop." Can you guess what George called the treat?

Frank made his treats by himself for two years. He sold seven flavors. In 1925, a company bought Frank's idea. Today, people eat millions of Frank's sweet treats. It all started with an 11-year-old boy!

1. Why did Frank's drink freeze?

_____

2. What two machines did Frank make?

_____

3. What did George name Frank's invention?

_____

☀ Reflect

What happened in 1925? How did this event change frozen treats?

_____

_____

_____

_____

Name _____

Read. Then, answer the questions.

Be Amazing

Kids do some **amazing** things, and you can too! Kids all over the world do amazing things.

Everyone has a talent. The things you like to do are clues. You can learn to be good at things. Start with the things you like to do.

Do you love to paint? Do you love to draw? You could take art lessons. Go to an art show. Talk to the artists. Take a pad of paper with you any place you go. Draw the things you see.

Maybe you love math. There might be an older child who could teach you about math. You could help tutor younger kids. You can learn a lot from being a student, and you can learn a lot from teaching someone else!

Would you like to work with animals? Help out at an animal shelter. You could talk to a vet. Maybe you could visit a farm, and you could learn from the farmer.

Maybe you want to help people. There are a lot of things kids can do. They can collect clothes for the homeless. They can collect food for food banks. Find a way to help. Start today!

So, do not be afraid. Find your gift. Look inside yourself. Be proud. You can do amazing things. All you have to do is learn, try, and do!

1. What does *amazing* mean?

_____

2. How can you learn what your talent is?

_____

3. What is another word for *teach*?

_____

Reflect

What can kids do to help people?

_____

_____

Name _____

Read. Then, answer the questions.

Exploring the Arctic

The Arctic is filled with danger. Many people wanted to be the first to stand at the North Pole. More than 800 explorers died trying to get there.

An explorer named Robert Peary thought his team could make it. He felt good because Matthew Henson was with them. Henson was a guide and explorer. He worked for Peary. Henson had spent years learning about the Arctic. He knew how to build igloos and hunt for food in the snow. He knew how to drive a dogsled team.

In 1908, Peary said his team would try one more time. He insisted that Henson go with the team. Peary was sure they could not make it without Henson. So, Matthew Henson prepared for another trip to the frozen Arctic.

Henson took great care to plan their trip. This time, they left food in igloos along the way. They would eat this food on the way back. Henson was the best dogsled driver on the team. He led the way. He made a trail for the rest.

On April 6, 1909, Matthew Henson stopped his sled. He did not need to go any farther. Henson, Peary, and their crew were at the North Pole. They were the first people to **triumph** over this world of ice and snow.

1. What does *triumph* mean?

_____

2. How were Robert Peary and Matthew Henson connected?

_____

3. What happened on April 6, 1909?

_____

☀ Reflect

Why was Henson so important? Underline clues in the story.

_____

_____

Name _____

Read. Then, answer the questions.

Digging for Dinosaurs

When you think about dinosaurs, do you think about Canada? You should! One of the best places to find dinosaur bones is in the province of Alberta, Canada. It is the Dinosaur Provincial Park, and it is found in a large valley. The valley was made at the end of the last ice age. The melting ice cut into the ground. It made a rock-filled river.

The area used to be warm. It had a lot of water. The ground was swampy. It was a great place for dinosaurs to find food. Scientists know this because they have found so many dinosaur bones there. Scientists have found at least 150 whole dinosaur skeletons! They have also found big piles of dinosaur bones. These are called bone beds.

There is one bone bed that has only **Centrosaurus** bones in it. These huge dinosaurs lived in herds. Scientists think a lot of members of a herd drowned there. Today, scientists are still finding many bones there.

Scientists have found the bones of at least 38 different types of dinosaurs in the park. Scientists have also found leaves from plants that once grew. The fossils in Canada's Dinosaur Provincial Park can teach us about the past.

1. Where is one of the best places to find dinosaur bones?

_____

2. What did Dinosaur Provincial Park look like in the past?

_____

3. What is a *Centrosaurus*?

_____

☀ Reflect

How many different types of bones have scientists found? What does this tell them?

_____

_____

Name _____

Read. Then, answer the questions.

The Amazing Amazon

The Amazon River in South America is a mighty force. Freshwater flows into the Earth's oceans. About 20 percent of it comes from this river. There is one river that is longer than the Amazon. It is the Nile River in Africa.

The Amazon has a lot of curves. Its source is high in the Andes Mountains. Its water flows more than 4,000 miles (6,437.38 km) to get to the sea.

People have not changed the Amazon much. There is a rain forest around it. Very few people live there. The rain forest trees are being cut down. But, there is not one bridge across the Amazon River.

A lot of **unique** creatures live in the Amazon River. A type of freshwater river dolphin lives there. Catfish there can weigh up to 200 pounds (90.72 kg)! Piranha live in the river too. These scary fish have sharp teeth.

An anaconda is a type of snake. It lives in the rain forest. It is one of the biggest snakes in the world. It floats just under the top of the water.

Thousands of rare creatures live in the rain forest. They each help make the Amazon River the awesome place that it is.

1. What does *unique* mean?

_____

2. Where is the source of the Amazon?

_____

3. What is shown in the picture?

_____

☀ Reflect

Why does the author feel that people have not changed the Amazon much?

_____

_____

Name _____

Read. Then, answer the questions.

Talk to the Animals

Dylan Scott Pierce was two years old when he started to draw. He loved to draw lions and dinosaurs. A lot of kids like to draw. But, Dylan was not the same. His pictures looked **lifelike**. Dylan won an art prize when he was nine years old. When he was 10, people bought his work. Some of his paintings sold for $20,000!

Dylan was schooled at home. This gave him time for his art. He also takes photos. He uses them when he plans a painting.

Dylan had not seen animals in their habitats. He went to Africa in 2003. Dylan went on safari. He saw all kinds of animals. Baboons jumped on his roof. He saw a herd of giraffes. An elephant chased them! Dylan painted a picture of the elephant. It showed how proud and free the animal was in its own home. Dylan could not have done that painting after going to a zoo.

Dylan liked his trip. He went to Africa again. This time, he saw lions. Dylan had painted lions for years. This was not the same. One lion looked him right in the eyes! This trip was more than five weeks long. Dylan uses some of the money he makes to help the people and animals of Africa.

1. What does *lifelike* mean?

_____

2. When did Dylan go to Africa?

_____

3. Which animal looked Dylan right in the eyes?

_____

 **Reflect**

What is Dylan Scott Pierce famous for?

_____

_____

Name _____

Read. Then, answer the questions.

Once Upon a Time

When a machine is first made, it is a breakthrough. No one has ever thought of it. It changes people's lives. But, new ideas do not stay new. Other inventions take their places.

Before 1450, books were **rare**. They were written by hand. If you wanted a book, you had to wait a long time. It could take years to make one book. Then, a man named Johannes Gutenberg changed things. He figured out a way to make type. The type was made out of wooden blocks. Gutenberg carved letters into the blocks. Then, he fitted them into a frame. The printing press machine put ink against paper. In 1452, he made 200 books. People were amazed. Today, we can print a lot of books at once. Computers make printing faster.

Today, computers are extreme machines. There are people who can recall life before computers. Now, computers are everywhere. They help run cars. They keep track of our files. They fly airplanes. They cook food. One day, people will look back. Today, the abacus seems old. The printing press does too. One day, even computers will seem old.

1. What does *rare* mean?

_____

2. How were books written before 1450?

_____

3. Who was Johannes Gutenberg?

_____

 **Reflect**

Why are computers "extreme machines"?

_____

_____

Name _____

Read. Then, answer the questions.

A National Treasure

Yellowstone National Park is in the western United States. Rivers, hot pools, and geysers are there. The Yellowstone volcano is there. A huge **crater** is there. It was left by the last volcano eruption. Earth's crust is very thin there. It is thinner than it is in other places.

A lot of geysers are in the park. No other place has more geysers. Old Faithful is the most famous geyser there. It erupts about every 90 minutes. Some other geysers are named Plume, Beehive, Castle, and Daisy.

There are other sights to see in Yellowstone. There are mountains, valleys, a canyon, and a huge lake. Yellowstone Lake is the largest mountain lake in the United States. The Grand Canyon of Yellowstone is a large, rocky canyon with a 308-foot (93.88 m) waterfall on one end. Herds of elk, packs of wolves, and families of moose roam through the valleys.

In 1872, Yellowstone was chosen to be the first US national park. It offers many natural wonders that cannot be seen anywhere else in the world.

1. What is a *crater*?

_____

2. What is the most famous geyser?

_____

3. When does it erupt?

_____

 **Reflect**

Why was Yellowstone chosen as the first national park?

_____

_____

_____

Name _____

Read. Then, answer the questions.

Americans in History

The United States of America is more than two hundred years old. Americans celebrate the country's birthday each year on the Fourth of July, or Independence Day. Two important Americans were George Washington and Thomas Jefferson.

George Washington was the first US president. He led many battles. There is a legend about George Washington as a little boy. It was said that he could not tell a lie. The story says little George cut down a cherry tree. When he was asked if he did it, he tried to lie, but he could not. George Washington was an honest man. Maybe that is why he was chosen to be on the one-dollar bill.

Thomas Jefferson was another president. In 1776, Jefferson wrote the Declaration of Independence that helped start the United States. He became the third president of the United States in 1801.

1. How old is the United States?

_____

2. Who was George Washington?

_____

3. Who was Thomas Jefferson?

_____

☀ Reflect

How are the second and third paragraphs similar?

_____

_____

_____

_____

Name _____

Read. Then, answer the questions.

The Huge Hunter

The polar bear lives in the coldest place on Earth. Its body keeps it warm. The polar bear has fur all over. Even its paws have fur on them. You might think a polar bear's fur is white. It is not! It is clear. It looks white because it reflects the sun's light. Each hair is hollow. The fur holds the sun's heat. The polar bear has black skin and a thick layer of fat.

The polar bear hunts on the snow. It has huge claws. The claws keep the bear from slipping. The polar bear also hunts in the water. It is a good diver. It can see under the water. On the ice, the polar bear can be patient and still. The polar bear looks for an airhole that a seal has made in the ice. It can wait beside one of these holes for hours. When the seal pokes its nose up to breathe, the bear grabs it. It pulls it onto the ice. Seals are the main part of the polar bear's diet. But, it is getting harder for polar bears to hunt.

Experts say that global warming is changing the polar bear's home and habits. The ice in the Arctic is thinner. The polar bear needs the ice to hunt seals for food. Experts are watching the polar bears. They are watching the warm weather. They wonder if the polar bears can **survive**.

1. What animal is part of a polar bear's diet?

_____

2. What does *survive* mean?

_____

3. Look at the picture and read the first paragraph. Describe a polar bear.

_____

Reflect

Why does the author think the polar bear's home is changing?

_____

_____

Name _____

Read. Then, answer the questions.

Friend or Enemy?

What does a cat do when it catches a mouse? It has a meal, right? Not always! Once, there was a cat named Huan. She had chased mice her whole life. She had always eaten them. But, once she caught a baby mouse. She did not kill it. She became friends with it!

People called the mouse Jerry. The two friends played together. They slept in the same bed. They drank water from the same bowl. Huan kept other cats away from Jerry. Jerry cleaned Huan's paws.

What is going on here? How could a cat and a mouse become friends?

This strange twist happens from time to time. No one knows why. Once, the owners of a park in Arizona planned a test. They chose animals that should not be friends. They chose mountain lions, gray wolves, and black bears. They put them together in one part of the park. Would they hurt each other? The owners thought they would not. They were right. A female wolf took the lead. She went to the mountain lions. She let them sniff her. Soon, these **enemies** were playing together. Then, the wolf made friends with the bears. Why did it turn out so well? No one knows.

1. What did people call the mouse?

_____

2. What are *enemies*?

_____

3. Look at the picture and read the second paragraph. Describe Jerry and Huan's friendship.

_____

_____

☀ Reflect

How are the animals in the Arizona Park like Huan and Jerry?

_____

_____

Read. Then, answer the questions.

Catch Me If You Can!

Many animals on the African grassland hunt their food. Those that do not want to be eaten have to run. The cheetah seems to know this. It is the fastest land animal on Earth. A cheetah can go from standing still to running fast in just three steps. In fact, a cheetah can run 40 miles (64.37 km) to 70 miles (112.65 km) per hour!

The cheetah is a good hunter. It has to guard the food it kills. Large animals, such as lions, might take the meat. Then, the cheetah has no food that day. It cannot hunt twice in one day. It has to rest after running so fast.

A mother cheetah shows her young how to hunt. She hurts a small animal. Then, she brings it to her cubs. She gives them the chance to chase and grab it. The cubs play games. The games help them run fast. They play tag, and they wrestle. The cubs will be good hunters in about three years.

After the cubs grow up, the females leave. They go off on their own. They have their own cubs. Brother cheetahs might stay together for life. They work as a team to hunt. They choose a **territory**. That is where they hunt. They protect the land together.

1. What is a *territory*?

_____

2. What is the fastest land animal on Earth?

_____

3. How does the mother cheetah show her young how to hunt?

_____

✸ Reflect

Why does the author think the cheetah is a good hunter?

_____

_____

Name _____

Read. Then, answer the questions.

Tornado Tips

    A tornado begins over land with strong winds and thunderstorms. The air begins to spin. It can cause damage. If you are inside, go to the lowest floor. A basement is a safe place. A bathroom or closet in the middle of a building can be a safe place too. If you are outside, lie in a ditch. Remember, tornadoes are dangerous.

1. Where does a tornado begin?

_____

2. What happens to the air?

_____

3. Look at the picture and read the paragraph. Describe a tornado.

_____

_____

 **Reflect**

Why are tornados dangerous?

_____

_____

Name _____

Read. Then, answer the questions.

Fish Can Protect Themselves

Most fish have ways to protect themselves from danger. Two of these fish are the triggerfish and the porcupine fish. The triggerfish lives in the ocean. When it sees danger, it swims into its hole. It puts its top fin up and squeezes itself in tight. Then, it cannot be taken from its hiding place. The porcupine fish also lives on the ocean. When danger comes, it puffs up like a balloon by swallowing air or water.

1. Which two fish does the author write about?

_____

2. What does a triggerfish do when it sees danger?

_____

3. What does a porcupine fish do when it sees danger?

_____

☀ Reflect

How are the two fish similar and different?

_____

_____

_____

Name _____

Read. Then, answer the questions.

Sharks Are Fish Too!

Addie learned a lot about sharks when her class visited the city aquarium. She learned that sharks are fish. Some sharks are as big as elephants, and some can fit into a small paper bag. Sharks have no bones. They have hundreds of teeth, and when they lose them, they grow new ones. They eat animals of any kind. Whale sharks are the largest of all fish.

1. How big are some sharks?

_____

2. What do they eat?

_____

3. How many teeth do sharks have?

_____

Reflect

Why did the author write this passage?

_____

_____

_____

_____

Read. Then, answer the questions.

Whales

Sleeping Whales

Whales do not sleep like we do. They take many short naps. Like us, whales breathe air. Whales live in very cold water, but they have fat that keeps them warm.

Singing Whales

Some whales can sing! We cannot understand the words. But we can hear the tune of the humpback whale. Each season, humpback whales sing a different song.

1. How do whales sleep?

   _____

2. What do whales breathe?

   _____

3. When do humpback whales sing different songs?

   _____

Reflect

How are the two paragraphs different?

_____

_____

_____

_____

Name _____

Read. Then, answer the questions.

Heavy Hitters

In 1998, Mark McGwire played for the St. Louis Cardinals. He liked to hit home runs. On September 27, 1998, he hit home run number 70. He set a new record for the most home runs hit in one season! The old record was set in 1961 by Roger Maris. Maris later played for the St. Louis Cardinals (1967 to 1968). With that team, he hit 61 home runs.

Other players are known for home runs too. Babe Ruth hit 714 home runs in his life. Baseball players keep swinging for the fence. Maybe someone will break the record again.

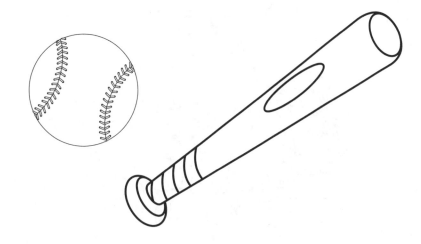

1. What team did Mark McGwire play for?

_____

2. What did he like to do?

_____

3. What is Babe Ruth known for?

_____

 Reflect

The passage says that players are "swinging for the fence." What does that mean?

_____

_____

Name _____

Read. Then, answer the questions.

Little Animals

Baby cats are called kittens. They love to play and drink a lot of milk. Baby dogs are called puppies. Puppies chew on shoes. They run and bark. Baby sheep are called lambs. Lambs eat grass. Baby ducks are called ducklings. Ducklings swim with their wide, webbed feet. Baby horses are called foals. Foals can walk the day they are born! Baby goats are called kids. Some people call children kids too!

1. What are baby cats called?

_____

2. What are baby dogs called?

_____

3. What do lambs eat?

_____

☀ Reflect

How are children similar to the young animals in the passage?

_____

_____

_____

Name _____

Read. Then, answer the questions.

Transportation

People use many kinds of transportation. Boats float on the water. Some people fish on boats. Airplanes fly in the sky. Flying in an airplane is a fast way to get somewhere. Trains run on tracks. The first car is the engine. The last car is the caboose. Some people even sleep in beds on trains! A car has four wheels. Most people have cars. Cars ride on roads. A bus can hold many people. A bus rides on roads. Many children ride buses to school.

1. What do some people do on boats?

_____

2. What does a train have?

_____

3. What can a bus hold?

_____

Reflect

What kind of transportation would be best to get you to another state? Why?

_____

_____

_____

_____

Name _____

Read. Then, answer the questions.

Two Holidays

The Chinese New Year is a very important holiday. It has been celebrated for thousands of years. It lasts for 15 days. There are many fireworks displays. There are parades at the end of the holiday. They are called dragon parades.

Americans celebrate the Fourth of July every year because it is the birthday of the United States of America. On July 4, 1776, the United States got its independence from Great Britain. Today, Americans celebrate this holiday with parades, picnics, and fireworks as they proudly wave the red-white-and-blue American flag.

1. How long does the Chinese New Year last?

_____

2. What are the Chinese New Year parades called?

_____

3. When did the United States get independence?

_____

Reflect

How are the Chinese New Year and the Fourth of July similar?

_____

_____

_____

_____

Name _____

Read. Then, answer the questions.

Bats

Many people are afraid of things they do not know much about. That is why so many people are afraid of bats. People who have learned about bats are not afraid of them. They realize that bats are not harmful. They are, in fact, helpful.

Did you know that some bats eat insects? That is right! Bats help control the insect population by eating mosquitoes, gnats, and other pests. Not all bats eat insects. Some bats eat fruit. They are called fruit bats.

Even though bats are our friends, it is not a good idea to try to pet or catch a bat. Even the most helpful animals will bite if they are scared. Some animals carry diseases, and they can give the diseases to people if they bite. If you see a bat, it is OK to look. But, do not touch!

1. What do some bats eat?

_____

2. What may animals do if they are scared?

_____

3. What should you do if you see a bat?

_____

☀ Reflect

Why does the author think that people are afraid of bats?

_____

_____

_____

Name _____

Read. Then, answer the questions.

The Koala

Have you ever seen a koala? You can find koalas eating leaves from special kinds of trees. They are called eucalyptus trees. They are in Australia.

Many people think koalas are bears because they look cute and cuddly like bear cubs. Koalas are not bears. They are **marsupials**.

Marsupials are special kinds of mammals. They have fur. They give birth to live babies. They get milk from their mothers. Koalas, like other marsupials, have pouches where their babies go to stay warm and safe.

1. What leaves do koalas eat?

_____

2. Where do koalas live?

_____

3. What are *marsupials*?

_____

☀ Reflect

What would you say if a friend called koalas "koala bears"? Why?

_____

_____

_____

Name _____

Read. Then, answer the questions.

Amazing Ants

Ants are everywhere. The only places where you will not find ants are places where it is so cold that snow and ice are there all year. Places such as Antarctica and the Arctic do not have ants.

There are thousands of different types of ants. Most ants, however, have a lot of things in common. Like other insects, ants have three main body parts: a head, a thorax, and an abdomen. They also have six legs.

The way ants work together and how they live is interesting. Ants are also very strong and work hard. Ants are amazing insects!

1. Where do ants live?

_____

2. What places do not have ants?

_____

3. How many types of ants are there?

_____

☀ Reflect

Look at the picture and read the second paragraph. Why are ants insects?

_____

_____

_____

_____

Name _____

Read. Then, answer the questions.

Cows Give Us Milk

Cows live on farms. Farmers milk the cows to get milk. Many things are made from milk. We make ice cream, sour cream, cottage cheese, and butter from milk.

Butter is fun to make! You can learn to make your own butter. First, you need cream. Put the cream in a jar and shake it. Then, pour off the liquid. Next, put the butter in a bowl. Add a little salt and stir! Finally, spread it on crackers and eat!

1. Where do cows live?

_____

2. Who milks the cows?

_____

3. What is made from milk?

_____

☀ Reflect

Look at the picture and read the second paragraph. Why does the author use a lot of exclamation points?

_____

_____

Name _____

Read. Then, answer the questions.

Germs

Have you ever heard someone ask you to please cover your mouth when you sneeze or cough? Do you know why you should do that? It is to keep germs that you have from spreading to other people. Germs are not something we can see, but when they get into our bodies, they can make us sick. Germs can travel in a lot of ways.

There are many ways to protect your body from germs. You should wash your hands with soap several times a day, especially before meals, after using the bathroom, and after coughing or sneezing. It is also smart to keep your own germs to yourself. You can do this by not sharing your food or drink with others, and by keeping your fingers out of your nose and mouth.

1. Why should you cover your mouth when you cough or sneeze?

_____

2. When should you wash your hands?

_____

_____

3. How can you keep your own germs to yourself?

_____

_____

Reflect

What can germs do to people?

_____

_____

Name _____

Read. Then, answer the questions.

How to Make Clay

It is fun to work with clay. Here is what you need to make it:

1 cup salt
2 cups flour
3/4 cup water

Mix the salt and flour. Then, add the water. Do not eat the clay. It tastes bad. Use your hands to mix and mix. Now, roll it out. You can make many things with clay. You can make shapes. You can make "people." You can make a "cat." You can even make a clay castle!

1. What is the title of the passage?

_____

2. How much flour do you need?

_____

3. Why should you not eat the clay?

_____

 **Reflect**

How is the picture helpful?

_____

_____

Name _____

Read. Then, answer the questions.

Warrior Queen

For 10 years, the army fought. It won the kingdom piece by piece. The head of the army was a woman. She wore armor and rode a white horse. She was a **warrior** and a queen. Her name was Isabella of Castile.

In the 1400s, women did not lead battles. Isabella was not a typical woman. She was not a typical queen. She ruled a piece of land. Her husband ruled another piece of land. They ruled with the same power. They went to war and took over a third piece of land. Today, the three kingdoms are Spain.

Isabella was brave. She liked things her own way. She set up schools. She made a big library of books and writings. Her son was schooled. But, she made sure her daughters were schooled too.

No woman during her time had the same kind of power. Isabella fought to unite Spain. She was not scared to rule. She was not scared to lead in a world led by men.

1. Who was the head of the army?

_____

2. What is a *warrior*?

_____

3. What are the three kingdoms called today?

_____

 **Reflect**

Why does the author describe Isabella as brave?

_____

_____

Name _____

Read. Then, answer the questions.

What Is Rain?

Clouds are made of little drops of ice and water. They push and bang into each other. Then, they join together to make bigger drops and begin to fall. More raindrops cling to them. They become heavy and fall quickly to the ground.

1. What are clouds made of?

_____

2. What do the little drops of ice and water do?

_____

3. How do they make bigger drops?

_____

☀ Reflect

Think about the title and the main idea. Compare them.

_____

_____

_____

_____

Name _____

Read. Then, answer the questions.

Animal Habitats

Animals live in different habitats. A **habitat** is an animal's natural home. Many animals live on land and others live in water. Most animals that live in water breathe with gills. Animals that live on land breathe with lungs.

A Bullfrog's Habitat

Each animal has a special habitat. A creek near some woods is a good habitat for a bullfrog. There are a lot of insects for the frogs to eat. There are also places for them to hide. The quiet water is a good place for them to lay their eggs. This habitat gives bullfrogs everything they need to live.

1. What is a *habitat*?

_____

2. What kinds of habitats do animals live in?

_____

3. Where do some bullfrogs live?

_____

☀ Reflect

How is the first passage different from the second passage?

_____

_____

_____

_____

Name _____

Read. Then, answer the questions.

Snakes

There are many facts about snakes that might surprise you. A snake's skin is dry. Most snakes are shy. They will hide from people. Snakes eat mice and rats. They do not chew them. Snakes' jaws drop open so that they can swallow their food whole.

Unlike people, snakes have cold blood. They like to be warm. They hunt for food when it is warm. They lie in the sun. When it is cold, snakes curl up.

1. What is a snake's skin like?

_____

2. Why do snakes hide from people?

_____

3. How do snakes eat food?

_____

☀ Reflect

How are snakes the same as and different from people?

_____

_____

_____

Name _____

Read. Then, answer the questions.

Quack, Quack!

Ducks were used during World War II. The first ducks were big, heavy trucks shaped like tanks. The huge trucks could take troops from a ship to the land. The trucks could carry **supplies** from land onto the water. They were big and slow. But, they helped keep the troops safe.

After the war, some people in the United States bought ducks. They were used to give rides. In a city such as Philadelphia, Pennsylvania, you can still ride in a duck. The duck takes you to sights on land. Then, it drives into the water!

It would be fun to own a sports-car duck. But, ducks are useful too. Some people think ducks could be ambulances. Some cities such as Seattle, Washington, have a lot of water and islands. A duck ambulance could save lives.

1. What are *supplies*?

_____

2. Where do ducks drive?

_____

3. What could a duck ambulance do?

_____

_____

☀ Reflect

How are ducks useful?

_____

_____

_____

Name _____

Read. Then, answer the questions.

Leaves

There are many different trees. Each kind of tree has a kind of leaf that grows on it. Examples of different leaves are below.

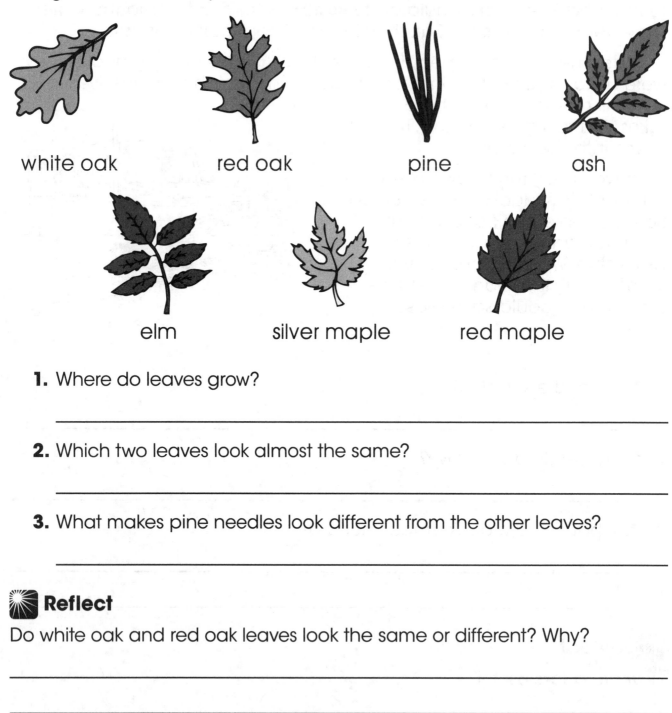

white oak   red oak   pine   ash

elm   silver maple   red maple

1. Where do leaves grow?

_____

2. Which two leaves look almost the same?

_____

3. What makes pine needles look different from the other leaves?

_____

☀ Reflect

Do white oak and red oak leaves look the same or different? Why?

_____

_____

_____

_____

Answer Key

Answers will vary but may include the answers provided. Accept all reasonable answers as long as students have proper evidence and support.

Page 5
1. supplies: a tent, three sleeping bags, three backpacks, and a cooler; 2. They put it with ice in a cooler. 3. in a tent

Page 6
1. a large amount of something, several; 2. a funny cousin; 3. It is a cake for many people.

Page 7
1. another person or a narrator; 2. unique, different; 3. It has wings, a tail, and horns.

Page 8
1. places a material over something; 2. She puts on her dad's big shoes and colors her nose red. 3. She likes it best.

Page 9
1. lies in the shade of the apple tree; 2. next to Bill; 3. an ant pulling on a leaf, a ladybug, a grasshopper, and a bee that lands on a flower

Page 10
1. work hard and do well; 2. all of the time; 3. It is always a good time to make friends.

Page 11
1. blue and red with white spots; 2. the wind was blowing; 3. up and up, high in the sky

Page 12
1. a boat out of a bar of soap; 2. happy and satisfied about what you have done; 3. It was sitting on the boat.

Page 13
1. a chopper toy; 2. Chesters; 3. happiness

Page 14
1. crossing guard; 2. cars, buses, and trucks; 3. It is a story because Bob might not be real.

Page 15
1. vet; 2. She helps sick pets. 3. She can help pets get well.

Page 16
1. white with a black spot around one eye; 2. gives him food and water and a warm place to sleep; 3. a dark circle

Page 17
1. another worker on a boat; 2. It is loud and gives a strong message. 3. the sea is no longer safe

Page 18
1. ran into the hen's pen; 2. run after and grab the pig; 3. food that pigs eat

Page 19
1. cute; 2. A pup's mother would be glad. 3. A cub's mother would be mad.

Page 20
1. a big pot; 2. the little man has it; 3. Josh was selfish. Then he was sorry, and he and the little man were nice to each other.

Page 21
1. zookeeper; 2. a fight; 3. One got a hurt paw, and the other got a sore jaw. Dawn took care of them.

Page 22
1. July; 2. a tune on her flute; 3. danced in her tutu

Page 23
1. to make a surprise breakfast for Mom and Dad; 2. breakfast: cereal with milk and toast with jam; 3. Mom and Dad

Page 24
1. tape; 2. a kite; 3. tape, a kite, a rope, and a dime

Page 25
1. He wanted to be in the big race, but he was too slow. 2. a pocket; 3. Sammy Snail

Page 26
1. the material on the surface of Earth; 2. space; 3. leapfrog on the moon

Page 27
1. 6 feet (1.83 m); 2. pulls leaves off of trees; 3. to watch over

Page 28
1. "Mom's Best White Cake"; 2. 1/2 cup; 3. 350°F

Page 29
1. 9-1-1; 2. stop, drop, and roll; 3. families

Page 30
1. weird or different; 2. It rained frogs and toads. 3. trout and catfish

Page 31
1. Frank left the glass outside in the cold overnight. 2. a machine to mold his snacks and a machine to stamp his name on the sticks; 3. ice pop

Page 32

1. wonderful, impressive; 2. Find something you like and are good at doing. 3. tutor

Page 33

1. win; 2. They were a team who worked together. 3. They arrived at the North Pole.

Page 34

1. the Dinosaur Provincial Park in Alberta, Canada; 2. It had a lot of water and swampy ground in a valley. 3. a huge dinosaur that lived in herds

Page 35

1. special; 2. high in the Andes Mountains; 3. the Amazon River in South America

Page 36

1. almost real, or looks like true life; 2. 2003; 3. a lion

Page 37

1. very hard to find; 2. by hand; 3. the man who invented the printing press

Page 38

1. a large hole in the ground; 2. Old Faithful; 3. every 90 minutes

Page 39

1. over 200 years old; 2. the first president of the United States; 3. the third president of the United States

Page 40

1. seal; 2. to stay alive; 3. It is covered in clear, hollow fur all over, has black skin, and has a layer of fat.

Page 41

1. Jerry; 2. people or animals that cannot get along; 3. They are great friends. They sleep in the same bed and drink from the same bowl. Huan keeps other cats away from Jerry. Jerry cleans Huan's paws.

Page 42

1. an area that an animal or group of animals lives in and protects; 2. the cheetah; 3. She hurts a small animal and brings it to her cubs to give them a chance to chase and grab it.

Page 43

1. over land with strong winds and thunderstorms; 2. It begins to spin. 3. A tornado is a dangerous storm in a funnel shape.

Page 44

1. the triggerfish and the porcupine fish; 2. It swims into its hole, puts its top fin up, and squeezes in tight. 3. It swallows air or water to puff up like a balloon.

Page 45

1. as big as elephants; 2. animals of any kind; 3. hundreds

Page 46

1. They take many short naps. 2. air; 3. in different seasons

Page 47

1. the St. Louis Cardinals; 2. hit home runs; 3. hitting 714 home runs in his lifetime

Page 48

1. kittens; 2. puppies; 3. grass

Page 49

1. Some people fish. 2. an engine and a caboose; 3. many people

Page 50

1. 15 days; 2. dragon parades; 3. July 4, 1776

Page 51

1. insects or fruit; 2. bite; 3. It is OK to look, but do not touch it.

Page 52

1. eucalyptus leaves; 2. Australia; 3. mammals that have pouches to keep their young in

Page 53

1. everywhere except Antarctica and the Arctic; 2. cold places with snow and ice all year; 3. thousands

Page 54

1. on farms; 2. farmers; 3. ice cream, sour cream, cottage cheese, and butter

Page 55

1. You do not want to spread germs to others. 2. several times a day, especially before meals and after using the bathroom; 3. By not sharing food or drink and keeping your fingers out of your nose and mouth.

Page 56

1. "How to Make Clay"; 2. two cups of flour; 3. It tastes bad.

Page 57

1. Isabella of Castile; 2. a person who fights in a battle and is known for courage or skill; 3. Spain

Page 58

1. little drops of ice and water; 2. push and bang into each other and then join together to make bigger drops; 3. They cling to each other.

Page 59

1. an animal's natural home; 2. land or water; 3. in creeks near woods

Page 60

1. dry; 2. They are shy. 3. They swallow their food whole.

Page 61

1. items that are needed for a group to survive; 2. on land and in water; 3. It could go over water to islands faster than a normal ambulance and save lives.

Page 62

1. on trees; 2. Answers will vary but may include elm and ash or white and red oak. 3. They look like sharp needles.